The Truth

BEHIND MY SMILE

The Truth

BEHIND MY SMILE

FROM BROKENNESS TO HEALING

Justine A. Cohen

Copyright © October 2020 by Justine A. Cohen

Printed in the United States of America

ISBN 978-976-655-053-0

Published by Justine A. Cohen

Rejoice not over me, O my enemy;
when I fall, I shall rise;
when I sit in darkness,
the Lord will be a light to me.
Micah 7:8 (ESV)

And we know that in all things God works
for the good of those who love him,
who have been called according to his purpose.
Romans 8:28 (NIV)

Contents

CONTENTS

Acknowledgment

Thank God for never leaving my side and giving me the courage I needed to share my story and allow it to help others.

I want to thank my mother, who despite our ups and downs, always saw the best in me. Even though her methods were unconventional at times, she always encouraged me to strive for the best, and I wouldn't be where I am today without her unending support.

To Bishop Christine Haber and the CHMI team, thank you for your constant support and encouraging words, especially in my difficult moments. The sermons and classes also gave me the motivation to consistently push through.

I want to thank all my friends who encouraged me when I told them what I was going to do and those who saw the book in me before I even got the revelation.

Special thanks to my friend Abigail Buchanan who introduced me to my writing coach's Instagram page and encouraged me to

ACKNOWLEDGMENT

stop overthinking and just make the investment to get my book started and completed.

Also, thanks to my some of my dearest friends: Shauna Isaacs, Alexis McConnell, Marsha-Gaye Knight, Marsha Lowe, Mickoy Porter and my Powerpuff Naturals (formerly Powerpuff Auditors) who were in support from day one and got more excited than I did about the book which fueled me to give this my all.

I am especially grateful for my writing coach, Sarita A. Foxworth, who gave me the jumpstart that ultimately resulted in this finished book.

Introduction

This book was written to encourage anyone who feels like they have stepped so far out of the will of God that there's no way He could possibly love them and still have a plan for them. The goal is to help people come to the realization that there is no place they can go that God will not find them and bring them back to Him.

Throughout the pages of the book, you will read about the many times I turned my back on God and did what "Justine" wanted and what "Justine" felt was best for her at the time. You will read about times when I put my will ahead of God's will for my life and how much pain and wasted time that caused me. In these same pages, you will also read about how God kept me and forgave me and continued to bless me because He knew the purpose He placed on my life. Like a gentleman, He was waiting for me to open my eyes and see myself the way He sees me.

The desire to write this book has been in my heart for close to three years now, and I allowed the fear of judgment and exposure of all my secrets to delay the process. At first, I also felt as if I needed the "happily ever after" ending before writing so that I could say to my readers that I got everything I ever wanted. I also allowed the enemy to speak dangerous words in my ear that disqualified me as a writer.

Throughout my life, anyone looking at me from the outside would see me smiling and in a good mood. If not, give me a few minutes and whatever upset me or got me down would wear off, and I would be back to smiling again. I seldom stayed in a funk too long unless it was something major. I was an expert at hiding how I truly felt from those around me. You wouldn't know something was up unless I chose to tell you.

The name of this book was birthed from that. I had reached a point in my life where people around me were starting to see the pain and hurt written all over my face. Though I would be smiling from ear to ear, as usual, people would ask if there was something wrong with me. It was then I realized that the pain was too much to handle, and I was unable to fake it anymore. The compilation of my life's events became just too much to bear. It was like boiling potatoes in a covered pot. When you initially put the pot on the heat, you never know what is going on inside. As time passes, the water begins to boil and bubble up, the steam rises, and the cover of the pot begins to move. Eventually, if the cover isn't lifted to release the pressure, the water starts to overflow and creates a big mess on the stove. I was the pot trying to keep the cover on with everything locked away on the inside, but the overflow was coming.

I can now say that my smiles are real and not a cover up, and I want that for every person who reads my story. I want to help you move from hopeless to hopeful! I will walk you through various stages of my life from childhood to adulthood and show how I fell down. I will also show how God still blessed me and share what God's Word has to say to help us in similar situations.

The following perfectly sums up my life—the lies I told myself and the freedom that comes from telling my truth, letting go, and letting God!

Lie number one: you're supposed to have it all together
And when they ask how you're doing
Just smile and tell them, "Never better"

Lie number two: everybody's life is perfect except yours
So, keep your messes and your wounds
And your secrets safe with you behind closed doors
Truth be told
The truth is rarely told, now
I say I'm fine, yeah, I'm fine oh I'm fine,
hey, I'm fine but I'm not
I'm broken
And when it's out of control
I say it's under control but it's not
And you know it

INTRODUCTION

I don't know why it's so hard to admit it
When being honest is the only way to fix it
There's no failure, no fall
There's no sin you don't already know
So let the truth be told...
Can I really stand here unashamed
Knowin' that you love for me won't change?
Oh God if that's really true
Then let the truth be told...

(Excerpt from "Truth be Told"
Songwriters: Matthew West / Andrew Pruis)

As the excerpt above states about our failures, let the truth be told. The Word of God states that we overcome by the word of our testimony. Sharing our truth is a step in the right direction toward freedom from the hold it has on our lives. Vulnerability leads to victory over our hurt and pain. When you open yourself up, the healing can begin.

They triumphed over him
by the blood of the Lamb
and by the word of their testimony;
they did not love their lives so much
as to shrink from death.
Revelation 12: 11 (NIV)

My prayer is that this book will give you the courage to do a couple of things. First, go to God in prayer, confess your sins, and welcome the Holy Spirit into your life. Second, ask God for the courage to open up and share your truth with someone you trust so that you can overcome.

It is a privilege to be forgiven and to be called a child of God.

Chapter 1

Who I Am

My name is Justine A. Cohen, and I was born in Kingston, Jamaica. I entered this world on June 14, 1985, at 5:55 a.m. My actual birth, according to my mother, was not a simple one. What started off as a natural birth ended up in an emergency cesarean section. I was a baby in distress. I guess I was eager to enter the world and got stuck trying to push my hands out with my head. I was told that the right side of my face and right arm were completely white from lack of blood and my right ear was folded over, but everything worked out well, and a beautiful 8 lb. 4 oz. baby was born. That was the start of this journey called life that I've been on for the last thirty-five years. Maybe if I knew what was ahead, I would have taken my time to enter the world.

The first few years of my life were wonderful. Although I grew up in a single parent home, my mother gave me everything I needed to succeed in life. I was also an only child for my mother and the last of four children for my father. Some people would call me spoiled, but I was a good child and got excellent grades in school, so I would say I earned it. My mother would expect nothing but excellence from me, which sometimes felt like pressure. I was always first or second in my classes, but every time there was a parent-teacher meeting, the number one complaint was that I talked too much in class. All my teachers in preparatory school would say, "Justine is such a smart child, but she finishes her work before the other children, then talks to them and wastes their time." My mother would always respond to them by saying that I needed to stop distracting the class but added that the other children should take responsibility and not allow me to waste their time. She said if no one spoke back to me, I would be forced to be quiet.

That was the truth. I always made friends everywhere I went and talking a lot is a trait I still have today. I can speak to new people fairly easily. The funny thing is, I always thought that I was a shy and reserved person, but I prove myself wrong almost daily. I am only shy when I have to speak to a large group or crowd.

My mother worked hard, and her job would take her out of town a lot. During the times she was away, I would stay with the housekeeper-nanny at our home, or as I grew older, I would stay with friends who went to the same school that I attended or with extended family. I would miss my mother a lot during those times, and I longed for her to come home. When I stayed home with the nanny, I would cry every day until she came back. However, when I stayed with friends or family, it was great for the first couple of days because I had the "siblings" that I didn't have at home. But as time passed, I was ready to go home. I think that my mother being away so much prevented us from getting as close as we could have been considering that it was just us in the house.

I started traveling to the United States of America at the age of three months and also went on multiple cruises with my family as a young girl. I think that is where my love for traveling and exploring new places began. I was truly blessed and had everything a child needed and more; however, there was one thing missing. My daddy wasn't there, and I always felt that void of not having him around. He was alive but didn't live with us. I didn't understand why until I was about twelve years old, and I had a lot of resentment toward him. He visited a couple of times while I was growing up, but I kept my distance as much as possible despite nudges from my mother to build a relationship with him. I needed my daddy to be there always and he wasn't. A couple of phone calls, infrequent monetary gifts, and random visits were not enough, so I stayed away when I could. Even though there were legitimate reasons for his physical absence, I always felt he could have done a better job at developing a relationship with me in my younger years.

I was also referred to as "the mistake" by one of my sister's friends, and that haunted me for years. Words have so much power, and we fail to recognize that on a daily basis. I would encourage everyone to watch the words you speak over your life and the lives of others. I was able to release myself from the power those words had over me through the love I received from my family. Also, as I got closer to Jesus, I learned that God makes no mistakes.

Kind words are like honey—
sweet to the soul and healthy for the body.
Proverbs 16:24 (NLT)

I eventually decided to set myself free from the bondage of unforgiveness and forgive my father for not being around. I started to build a relationship with him, but unfortunately, he became extremely sick shortly after and lost his battle with cancer. I was upset with myself because I had wasted so much time being angry at him and pushing him away in later years whenever he tried to talk to me. I had told myself it was too late. I was comforted by the fact, however, that I had started talking to him, and even though it was only for a short time, I was able to let go of the anger and be at peace.

Growing up without a father really does have an impact on young girls. Many people think it doesn't have an effect, but looking back at my life, I see the effects over and over again. I believe this is the reason that at a young age I was desperately searching for the love of a man—any man. I just wanted someone to tell me they loved me. I put pressure on men to give me the love that my daddy didn't provide. I had never gotten to experience an earthly father's love, see an example of it, or be taught how men should treat me. I never had a standard to hold a man up to, so I accepted anyone who came by and made me feel noticed and loved.

As an adult, I volunteered a couple times with a non-profit organization run by a couple from my church here in Florida where young girls are crowned as daughters of the King and are taught about God's love for them and how much He cares about every aspect of their lives. They are able to feel valuable and precious. I wish there had been something like that for me growing up. I am sure I would have made better decisions in life, but as you will read, God still used my mess to deliver His message. Also, my mother made sure I had a good Christian foundation, so even though I strayed, I knew the way I should go and ultimately returned.

> Train up a child in the way he should go,
> And when he is old he will not depart from it.
> Proverbs 22:6 (NKJV)

For those of you who have children, even if both parents are raising them, make sure to teach them about God's love for them. Each and every one of us are so special in His eyes, and no matter who forsakes us in this world, God promises to never leave us. He is always there for us, catching each tear and longing for us to call on Him and allow Him to take control of our lives. He sees us and He loves us.

Indeed, the very hairs of your head
are all numbered.
Don't be afraid;
you are worth more than many sparrows.
Luke 12:7 (NIV)

You keep track of all my sorrows.
You have collected all my tears in your bottle.
You have recorded each one in your book.
Psalm 56:8 (NLT)

For you created my inmost being;
you knit me together in my mother's womb.
I praise you because I am fearfully
and wonderfully made;
your works are wonderful, I know that full well.
My frame was not hidden from you
when I was made in the secret place,
when I was woven together
in the depths of the earth.
Your eyes saw my unformed body;
all the days ordained for me
were written in your book
before one of them came to be.
How precious to me are your thoughts, God!

WHO I AM

How vast is the sum of them!
Were I to count them,
they would outnumber the grains of sand—
when I awake, I am still with you.
Psalm 139:13-18 (NIV)

A Prayer for Your Child

Father, I come before You in the name of Jesus Christ, Your Son. I pray that my child will feel loved and valuable. Help me to teach them how precious they are in Your sight and how much of a gift they are to me. Help them to realize that they are fearfully and wonderfully made, and You are protecting them always. In Jesus' name, Amen!

Chapter 2

My Relationship with God Growing Up in Jamaica

As a child, I grew up in a Christian home and attended church almost every Sunday. I gave my life to the Lord at an Inter-School Christian Fellowship (ISCF) event in high school at fourteen years old, but I really did not connect with the Holy Spirit at that time, and I certainly did not fully walk the path of a Christian. Growing up I knew what the Word of God said about the path that I was to walk in. For example: I told everyone I was waiting for marriage to have sex, but the world took hold on me. Apart from going to church on Sundays, I was doing my own thing.

At the age of thirteen, I had a boyfriend that was about four years older than me—horrible idea, I know. My mother used to tell me that I was not allowed to speak to him, but my response was that I loved him, and she couldn't stop that love. As children, we have no idea how much we are lacking in wisdom, and I later found out the hard way that I should have listened to her.

I would find ways to see him. He would come by the house whenever she wasn't there. For the most part, the relationship was innocent until one day during a phone conversation, I made the mistake of running a joke about wanting to have sex. What I thought was just innocent flirting and playing around took a turn for the worst. The next time he came over, he forced himself on me sexually, and despite my cries for him to stop, I lost my virginity at fourteen years old. My innocence was robbed. He was a very jealous person, and during that same visit, he accused me of cheating on him with a friend; his anger caused him to hold my naked body at the top of the stairs, threatening to let go.

That situation traumatized me, and for the first time ever, I wanted to die. I was going to overdose on pills, but something stopped me. At that time, I had no idea what it was, but I suddenly felt a fear of taking my life. I immediately changed my mind and went to my room to cry. Looking back, I know that was God looking out for me; He saved my life.

Though I walk in the midst of trouble, you preserve my life.
You stretch out your hand against the anger of my foes;
with your right hand you save me.
Psalm 138:7 (NIV)

Despite the incident that occurred, I remained in the relationship. He apologized, and I forgave him. I was young and very afraid to leave him. I had tried to leave previously, and he slit his wrist while I was on the phone worrying as he described the blood dripping down his hand. He had a history of cutting himself, he carved his pet name for me in his arm during our relationship, so I believed him that night. I was very afraid of being around him even though I was technically still his girlfriend. One night he came by the house to see me when my mother wasn't home and I insisted that he had to stay outside, speaking to him only through the grill door. At one point, he said he needed to use the bathroom, and after he begged and pleaded with me, I let him in. Big mistake! He somehow got a knife from the kitchen and held me on the floor while I attempted to fight him off. I didn't mention it before, but he was over six feet tall, and I was a skinny little girl only about five feet tall. He pressed the knife against my wrist and threatened to slit it. That night I was terrified. I felt like I was stuck. I didn't tell my mother out of fear that I would be in trouble for disobeying her.

After he left that night, I was crying on the floor of my bedroom and my landline rang. Most people probably don't even remember landlines, but I had no cell phone at that age. The call was from a good friend of mine, calling to say hi, and after hearing my voice, he proceeded to ask what was wrong.

I told him everything. He was the first and only person for a number of years to know what I went through. He gave me the strength and support to walk away from that relationship. Looking back at that night, I know God prompted him to call me. He might not have been a Christian at the time, but God uses anyone as long as they are available. He can even use you! God is always present and looking out for His children.

> When you pass through the waters, I will be with you;
> and when you pass through the rivers,
> they will not sweep over you.
> When you walk through the fire, you will not be burned;
> the flames will not set you ablaze.
> Isaiah 43:2 (NIV)

After that incident, I decided I was definitely not going to have sex with anyone before marriage, and the relationship I had following the abusive one helped me to heal. The friend that saved me that night became my boyfriend and he was a gentleman and never forced me to do anything. It was at this time that I attended the Inter-School Christian Fellowship gathering and gave my life to the Lord. But as I mentioned earlier, my Christian walk was not in place because I had not grown in the Holy Spirit. I had begun attending a new church and learned more about the Lord in their Sunday school. I was very focused on keeping my "no sex before marriage" promise, and I was able to keep it through high school. I also was able to forgive my abuser. I couldn't bring myself to speak to him, but I didn't have any hatred in my heart toward him. Only by the grace of God was I able to forgive him at the time.

You can forgive someone and love them from a distance, as God has commanded us to love, but you don't have to be friends with them. His company would not have been good for me.

We need to assess the relationships in our lives, identifying the ones that tear us down and are not uplifting. Once we identify those, we need to pray for the courage to walk away from them. Dismiss the lie that if you walk away, you are not displaying God's love.

> Be kind to one another, tenderhearted,
> forgiving one another,
> as God in Christ forgave you.
> Ephesians 4:32 (ESV)

Prayer

Dear Heavenly Father, I thank You for Your protection. Even in the midst of my mistakes, You choose to look out for me and bless me. Thank you for Your forgiveness and Your new mercies every day. Your love is so unconditional! Please help me to love others the way You love and forgive as You have forgiven me so many times. Help me to experience the freedom of forgiveness. In Jesus' name, Amen.

Chapter 3

College Days

My initial plans were to finish the last two years of high school (6th form) and then attend college in the United States. I started the first year of 6th form, but after September 11, 2001, I decided I would not be moving again. The fear of living in America after the bombing crippled me. I immediately applied for the University of Technology, Jamaica, and left high school one year early. I started dating someone new, and he was my boyfriend for my entire college life. I was not pressured by him, but I jumped off the "wait for marriage" train and officially broke my virginity with him at the age of seventeen years old. During college, we partied a lot, drank (I was never a big drinker), and of course, had lots of sex. There were days I would leave school when I didn't have class, just to go be with him. Oh, to be young and "in love!"

Then it happened—something I could never imagine—I got pregnant. It all started out as a prank because my period was delayed, and when I finally saw blood, I decided to play a joke about being pregnant. Little did I know that I was only spotting, and I was, in fact, really pregnant. I didn't know what to do; I couldn't stop thinking about how disappointed my mother and entire family would be. I had just started college. I was nowhere close to finishing my degree and being a college dropout was not an option. I was supposed to be smarter than that and make right choices.

At this point in my life, I had no adult I could confide in, so the decision was left up to me and my boyfriend. I tried to find ways to "lose" the baby like drinking white cane vinegar which burned my throat like crazy. I don't remember where that idea came from because at that time Google wasn't very popular.

I felt I had no choice but to have an abortion and got a recommendation for a doctor who would perform the procedure. The day of the procedure, I was terrified, and a couple of our friends accompanied us to the doctor's office. I had thoughts of killing myself again and attempted to walk out into the busy road outside the doctor's office. I was stopped by one of my friends who grabbed me before I walked through the gate. Looking back, I believe that was God protecting me once more, even in the midst of my mess. The actual procedure is a blur, I was given an anesthetic, so I was unconscious for the duration. I woke up groggy and in some pain. All I wanted to do was sleep and forget this ever happened. I loved children; I still do. How could I have done that? That question haunted me for years.

The sad thing is, as much as that experience hurt me, I didn't learn my lesson. I allowed my flesh to control me over and over. Sex was like a drug to me, and even though I knew I was super fertile, I kept playing Russian roulette with my reproductive system. I was stuck in a cycle from which I couldn't break free and reaping the destruction from it.

Whoever sows to please their flesh, from the flesh will reap destruction; whoever sows to please the Spirit, from the Spirit will reap eternal life. Let us not become weary in doing good, for at the proper time we will reap a harvest if we do not give up.
Galatians 6:8-9 (NIV)

I am not proud of this, but I am sharing now because I have been redeemed, and I believe someone can learn from my failures. It took a while for me to get to the point of accepting the forgiveness God was freely giving me. Most times the hardest person to forgive is yourself. So, not only did I take some time to accept the forgiveness of God, but I also held on to the guilt and refused to forgive myself. The closer I got to Jesus, the more I felt free. Today I believe, despite my mistakes, God will bless me with the children He has promised me based on prophecies from a couple people I trust and my own confirmation from God years after the incident.

God will keep His promise even if we step out of His will and try to take matters into our own hands. His Word will never return to Him void.

Blessed is she who has believed
that the Lord would fulfill his promises to her!
Luke 1:45 (NIV)

Take delight in the Lord,
and he will give you the desires of your heart.
Psalms 37:4 (NIV)

So is my word that goes out from my mouth:
It will not return to me empty, but will accomplish what I desire
and achieve the purpose for which I sent it.
Isaiah 55:11 (NIV)

Consider the Abram/Abraham story; God had promised him a son, but he got impatient. He had Ishmael with his wife's slave. But even though he stepped out of the will of God, he eventually got the promised child Isaac. God has never, and will never, let you down. He will watch over His Word to perform it.

After this, the word of the Lord came to Abram in a vision: "Do not be afraid, Abram. I am your shield, your very great reward."
But Abram said, "Sovereign Lord, what can you give me since I remain childless and the one who will inherit my estate is Eliezer of Damascus?" And Abram said, "You have given me no children; so a servant in my household will be my heir."

COLLEGE DAYS

Then the word of the Lord came to him: "This man will not be your heir, but a son who is your own flesh and blood will be your heir." He took him outside and said, "Look up at the sky and count the stars—if indeed you can count them." Then he said to him, "So shall your offspring be."   Genesis 15:1-5 (NIV)

Now Sarai, Abram's wife, had borne him no children. But she had an Egyptian slave named Hagar; so she said to Abram, "The Lord has kept me from having children. Go, sleep with my slave; perhaps I can build a family through her."
    Abram agreed to what Sarai said. So after Abram had been living in Canaan ten years, Sarai his wife took her Egyptian slave Hagar and gave her to her husband to be his wife. He slept with Hagar, and she conceived.   Genesis 16:1-4 (NIV)

Then God said, "Yes, but your wife Sarah will bear you a son, and you will call him Isaac. I will establish my covenant with him as an everlasting covenant for his descendants after him. And as for Ishmael, I have heard you: I will surely bless him; I will make him fruitful and will greatly increase his numbers. He will be the father of twelve rulers, and I will make him into a great nation. But my covenant I will establish with Isaac, whom Sarah will bear to you by this time next year." When he had finished speaking with Abraham, God went up from him.   Genesis 17:19-22 (NIV)

To anyone out there who feels they have done the worst things in life, something seemingly unforgivable, please believe me when I say we can take God at His Word. His Word says that *He will never leave us nor forsake us (Deuteronomy 31:6).* There is absolutely NO SIN that Jesus' sacrifice on the cross doesn't cover. His sacrifice

19

suffices; *"Love covers a multitude of sins" (I Peter 4:8)*. All we have to do is humbly approach the throne of God in prayer and a posture of repentance.

God has forgiven me! He has set me free from the guilt and shame I carried deep down inside. I used to tell myself I would never have children because that was my punishment from God. I am so glad *"He doesn't treat us as our sins deserve" (Psalm 103:10)*. God is so full of grace and mercy! I want to encourage you that God will never run out of love and grace for His children. Nothing we do is unforgivable. NOTHING! And until I realized this, the enemy held me bondage with the memory of my sins, but God—

> ... does not treat us as our sins deserve
> or repay us according to our iniquities.
> For as high as the heavens are above the earth,
> so great is his love for those who fear him;
> as far as the east is from the west,
> so far has he removed our transgressions from us.
> Psalm 103:10-14 (NIV)

> Because of the Lord 's great love we are not consumed,
> for his compassions never fail.
> They are new every morning;
> great is your faithfulness.
> Lamentations 3:22-23 (NIV)

If you are in a place where you need a touch from the Lord and His forgiveness to lift that load from your shoulders, pray the following prayer.

Prayer for Forgiveness

Dear Heavenly Father, I pray in the name of Jesus Christ, please have mercy on your child. I thank you for loving me, God. Lord, I repent of all the sins I have committed, both known and unknown. Father, create in me a clean heart and renew a right spirit within me. Help me to be more like your Son each and every day. Cleanse me from the inside out. Help me to never return to my old ways and mistakes. Set my feet on higher ground, Mighty God. Lord, I lay my burdens at Your feet and take on Your yoke. In Jesus' name I pray, Amen!

Chapter 4

Moving to the U.S.—
Back to School and My
First Job

In 2008, I was a U.S. resident living in Jamaica, and after an interesting encounter with U.S. Immigrations at the Miami International Airport, I was forced to make the decision to move to the United States of America—Florida to be exact. I left my job with a Big 4 audit company and all my family and friends with no potential job or real plan. I literally took a leap of faith and hoped someone, preferably God, would catch me.

I moved to Florida in November of 2008, during the Great Recession—worst time to move to a new country with no savings and no job lined up. I was blessed enough to have family members to move in with, and I started the job hunt immediately. Days, weeks, and months passed; I experienced rejection after rejection. Even the Florida office of the Big 4 company I worked for in

Jamaica told me that they were on a hiring freeze and couldn't give me employment. I remember a particular encounter in which my recruiter was so excited for this potential job offer she had for me with a client. She was sure that with my experience and level of education, I was more than qualified for the position. Needless to say, she called me one day in anger and told me that the client refused to even consider me because I did not have a U.S. education or experience, and he would rather take someone straight out of college. I should point out that it was a position that had not required U.S. experience. That event hurt me to the core. In Jamaica, I would be considered a top choice because I had a college degree and years of experience at one of the international Big 4 audit companies. The recruiter tried to make me feel better by saying the guy was making a mistake and that she would no longer assist him in filling that position. Nice try, but it did not help. My spirit was crushed.

Despite how I felt, I still pushed and continued to send out what felt like a million résumés daily. All I received were generic responses from recruiters to meet with them, then they would search for job openings to fit. I got tired of getting dressed up to have mock interviews with all these recruiters only for it to lead nowhere. Most companies were on hiring freezes, and in my mind, those who were hiring did not want me, just like the man I previously mentioned.

This experience of rejection and frustration brought me closer to God. In 2009, I started attending a church my aunt had told me about that was known for their Christmas light displays and thriving youth membership. I immediately felt like I was home. A couple months later, I decided to re-dedicate my life to the Lord and get baptized (something I was ashamed to do in Jamaica for fear of judgment). I also started tithing even before obtaining a fulltime job, and I have been tithing ever since. I gave a tithe based on the little money I would receive from odd jobs like babysitting.

My relationship with God grew day by day, and in the midst of my search for employment, I felt a prompting to stop searching and go back to school. I felt like God was saying to me, "Give this to Me; I will take control now." So, I let go and let Him handle it. Please note, I had sworn upon leaving Jamaica that I would never go back to school; however, I have eaten those words many times in the last twelve years of living in Florida.

The decision to enroll in the Master's program was very last minute, and as such, I had to study and pass the GMAT examination in two weeks in order to receive and submit the results before the application period closed. Only God can explain how I was successful! As with all things, God wants to show us that He is the One making things happen and not us in our own strength. If I had had months to prepare for the exam, I would have taken the credit for passing, but in this situation, I can only say it was God. I was accepted to Florida Atlantic University to do my

Master's in Business Administration with an Accounting track. In my first semester, I could only do one course because I was still considered an out-of-state student (having been in Florida less than a year), and the out-of-state tuition was triple the in-state tuition.

My program was geared toward students already in the workforce, so our sessions were held in the evenings. One of my first friends in class told me she worked at a recruiting company. I got really excited and told her my job-hunting woes. The company, however, only did recruiting for temporary hospitality staff and did not handle accounting jobs. She mentioned their sister company that did more professional-type job recruitment and told me she would share my résumé with them. Even though I shared my résumé with her, I was still in the mindset that God was going to work it out, and I just needed to focus on school. Once again, God showed up.

My friend came to class one evening and asked me if I wanted her job! I was confused until she explained that she was leaving the company to work for one of the Big 4 audit firms. She said she would be happy to recommend me for the position if I wanted it. Please remember, she hadn't known me for more than maybe a month or two and only through the two to four hours a week in class, yet she felt the need to put herself on the line and recommend me. I went to the interview, and her boss was so impressed, he took me on a tour of the office and introduced me to everyone that same day, even showing me where I would sit. He didn't tell me upfront that I received the job, but my friend called me after I left and told me no one else got that treatment; she was almost one hundred percent sure I had the job. He had spoken to her and told her how much he liked me.

The next day, I received a call that I was being offered the job. God came through once more! I was excited and relieved. I had waited and had been living for almost a year in Florida before landing my first full-time job.

The blessings continued during my year at that job. I mentioned earlier that I only did one course in my first semester. I had taken a student loan to pay for it, much to my dismay, because I never wanted to have this debt to repay, but I had no choice at the time. The loan was $5,000 for that single three-credit graduate course, believe it or not. I was dreading having to apply for more money for the upcoming semester, even though I was now considered an in-state student (which I barely qualified for because I was off by a month or two, but God again showed up and gave me favor). With the in-state status, I would now pay approximately one-third of my first cost per course, but I still needed a loan.

Good News! I never had to apply for additional student loans. The company I started working with and the one that I transitioned to a year later both offered to pay my full tuition every semester as long as I kept a B average or higher, which I made sure to do. I can say that I have no outstanding student loans because even the $5,000 has been paid off. Glory to God!

MOVING TO THE U.S.

And my God will meet all your needs according to the
riches of his glory in Christ Jesus.
Philippians 4:19 (NIV)

Every good and perfect gift is from above,
coming down from the Father of the heavenly lights,
who does not change like shifting shadows.
James 1:17 (NIV)

Importance of Tithing

Many people don't believe in tithing because they say they don't trust the church. Others say they don't have enough money to tithe. I am a living testimony that tithing works. As I mentioned earlier, I started tithing even before I had a full-time job. I gave from the little I had, and I was blessed with more. I have been tithing consistently for over ten years now, and I have never been left lacking. My needs are always met! God always provides! There is also a joy that comes from giving to His kingdom. I honestly believe that the blessing of having my school fees paid was a result of my obedience in tithing, and that is just one of the many examples throughout my life. The Lord only wants 10%; we get to keep 90% for ourselves. This is the only area in which the Lord says to test Him. Try it out!

"Bring the whole tithe into the storehouse,
that there may be food in my house.
Test me in this," says the Lord Almighty,
"and see if I will not throw open the floodgates
of heaven and pour out
so much blessing
that you will not have room enough for it.
Malachi 3:10 (NIV)

MOVING TO THE U.S.

Give, and it will be given to you.
A good measure, pressed down, shaken together
and running over,
will be poured into your lap.
For with the measure you use,
it will be measured to you.
Luke 6:38 (NIV)

Prayer

Dear gracious Heavenly Father, I want to thank you for all the blessings you have bestowed upon me. Help me, Lord, to hand over the control of my life to you. Help me to actively let go and let You have Your way. Father, I pray that You give me the courage to step out in faith and begin tithing. Create in me a giving spirit. In Jesus' name, Amen!

Chapter 5

Dating in the U.S. After Baptism

Even after being baptized, I was still one foot in and one foot out with my relationship with God. I was what people would call a "lukewarm" Christian. It didn't help that my circle of friends, even though they believed in God and went to church occasionally, were not sold out to Christ. This made falling back into old habits and routines quite simple. I continued to go to parties and drink alcohol until I was almost drunk. I continued to date men that only wanted one thing, and I didn't fight it because I thought that's what I wanted and needed too. I truly just loved the feeling of having someone care about me and someone for me to care about and do almost anything for. I poured out one hundred percent every time, no matter what.

Of course, these relationships were short-term; as one ended another one started. The ultimate goal of these relationships was sex and companionship. There was no long-term plan of getting married and building a life together, and of course, there was definitely no talk about fulfilling God's purpose in our lives.

The cycle continued. During this period of my life, I continued to attend church, but that was basically it. I was just an attender. I often felt the urge to get involved and serve in children's ministry, but I knew I was still living a sinful life, so I told myself that I couldn't serve until I got married one day.

In hindsight, at that early stage in my walk, I needed to surround myself with fellow believers to hold me accountable so I would not fall back into the familiar ways of the world.

Somewhere in all of this, I started dating my friend from college as a result of some of our mutual friends suggesting we take a chance and date. During the two years of dating, we were in a long-distance relationship, something I swore to myself that I would never get into, especially with a Jamaican man. However, he had been a good friend for so many years. He knew all the stories of heartbreak from previous boyfriends and gave such good advice about what to look for in a man and what not to accept. I thought he was perfect and would be the best person for me.

The dating years were great, or so I felt at the time. I visited every couple months, and he would also come to Florida. He would attend church with me during his visits but wouldn't go to church once he returned home. We spoke about getting married someday after maybe a year of dating, and I remember telling him that my Christianity was especially important to me. I told him I would need him to attend church with me, to which he said he would sometimes. I knew this wasn't an equally yoked union, but like many of us, I found ways to justify my decision to stay with him and follow through with marriage in the future.

My picture of Christianity at that time was just making sure I wasn't committing sin. In my head, my only sin at the time was fornication and that would all be fixed once I got married. I was so misled and horribly incorrect. I always thought that I couldn't fully serve God and fulfill my purpose until I was married. Like almost every young girl, I always dreamt of getting married and having all my children before the age of thirty. I bought into what society taught me as a young girl that getting married and having children would be what made me complete and whole as a woman. Also, as I mentioned earlier, I didn't grow up with a father in the house. I didn't want that for my children, so getting married before having kids was always something I wanted.

Let no one deceive you with empty words, for because of such things God's wrath comes on those who are disobedient.
Ephesians 5:6 (NIV)

TRUTH BEHIND MY SMILE

Save me, Lord, from lying lips
and from deceitful tongues.
Psalm 120:2 (NIV)

But Samuel replied:
"Does the Lord delight in burnt offerings and sacrifices
as much as in obeying the Lord?
To obey is better than sacrifice,
and to heed is better than the fat of rams."
1 Samuel 15:22 (NIV)

Prayer

Dear gracious Heavenly Father, I come to You in the name of Jesus Christ, Your Son, and I repent of my sin of disobedience. Save me from the tongues of deceit that pull me away from obeying You. Your Word says obedience is better than sacrifice. Forgive me Lord, for not trusting You enough with my life to obey Your Word. Help me to tune in only to Your voice, Father. I declare that I am free from the spirit of disobedience, and I will be intentionally walking in obedience to You, Lord. In Jesus' name I pray, Amen!

Chapter 6

Marriage

In 2013, after dating my boyfriend for two years, we decided to do something quick and get married so that I could start working on the paperwork to get him to the United States. The plan was to do the "real" wedding ceremony and reception the following year after saving some money. Deep inside of me something didn't feel right, number one being he wasn't a Christian, and I knew it. But like many Christian women, I told myself that I would continue to pray for him; God would change him, and things would be awesome. I'm not saying it isn't possible for a man to change; however, since I was a Christian before getting married, I was wrong to be unequally yoked with someone. I realized this even then, but once again, I took my timeline and ignored God's plans. I was already twenty-eight years old; according to my timeline, I should have been married three years prior, so I was running late! There was no time to wait on what God had prepared for me; I was in love. It felt eighty-five percent right. I thought it couldn't be that bad—God honors marriage, and now I would be "legally" having sex. It could only go up from there, right?

Sometimes I think God looks down at me making my own decisions and ignoring His voice, holds His head in His hands, and thinks to Himself—when will My child ever learn to just trust that I know what is best for her.

We got married in the presence of three friends and two pastors at a beautiful location upon a hill with a great view in St. Catherine, Jamaica. Then we left for the honeymoon, just a night at a hotel in Ocho Rios, Jamaica. Though it was fun and I felt happy, I had to hide that I was married from most people because we were planning a "real" wedding. This was rough, but I had agreed to it, so I had to follow through.

This worked perfectly in my husband's favor because he could go back to living as if he weren't married. Also, I was living in another country, so he just went back to life as it was. I would spend a lot of time calling and trying to reach him because he would go missing for hours. I longed for the day when he would be with me so I wouldn't have the frustration of not being able to talk to him when I wanted to.

The immigration process took about eighteen months to be completed, with me taking care of everything. I paid all the fees and filled out every form. All he had to do was get his medical examination done and show up at the embassy for the interview. Everything was sorted out by May of 2015. I was excited because the following month was my birth month, and I would finally have my husband living with me.

However, my husband was not as excited and took almost five months to move. He was in no rush to get here and gave me excuse after excuse. U.S. Immigration gives you six months to get everything in order before moving, and he made sure to use almost all of the allotted time. I moved to the U.S. in 3 months or less, and that was without any prior mental preparation, yet he had known this was coming for eighteen months. Clearly, I was not very understanding and got upset with his delay.

When he got here, things immediately went south. First, you would think that he would be excited to see his wife, but I was the only one excited. It was like night and day; there was a distance between us that got worse as time passed. We had our fun moments, but more than half the time, I felt alone in my marriage. I have the notes and messages I wrote to him asking him what was wrong and why he felt so distant. We argued quite a bit and the promise to attend church with me flew out the door. The person I had known as a friend and then my long-distance boyfriend and finally husband, was not the same person I was now living with.

They have this saying in Jamaica: "See mi and come live wid mi a two different tings," which means knowing someone and actually living with them is quite different. Yes, we had our arguments about the mess he left with his clothes in the room or the way the towel was left on the bed, but these weren't what made him a different person. The person that I thought would do anything to make me happy, the one who made me feel loved and cared for, wasn't showing up like he used to. I started to question if it hadn't been real. Perhaps now that he was around me for longer than our regular visits of a week or two, he could no longer pretend.

I often asked him if he no longer wanted to be with me, even telling him many times to just leave instead of causing me pain. Of course, he would turn it all on me, and say I was pushing him out. Also, the "real" wedding that I was hoping would happen, never did. In hindsight, at least I saved that money.

When we were dating, my husband had said he wanted us to have a child. I told him we had to wait until we were married because I had promised myself I would never have a child out of wedlock. After being married for a year or two, I suggested that we could try to have a baby, but he was no longer interested. He also made sure there were no slip-ups at all.

I always found it strange that when I was younger, I got pregnant so easily, but now, when I was no longer on birth control, nothing happened. I prayed and asked God if this was my punishment for the abortion. I questioned why He was doing this to me. I had received more than one prophecy about a son I would give birth to, but as time passed, I questioned the Lord's promise to me. I was devastated every time a friend would get pregnant because I wanted a child so badly, and He had promised me I was going to give birth. I would cry and be angry with God, pleading with Him to bless me with my child so I could be happy.

Just two years ago, I received the revelation that the Lord had probably closed my womb during this period, for which I am grateful. I don't think our situation was conducive to bringing a child into our lives at that time.

Throughout the years, things got worse instead of better. My husband would stay away from the house until late most evenings of the week and not answer his phone ninety percent of the time after leaving his office. He expected me to make dinner every night but sometimes did not come home until after 10 p.m. Then he said it was too late for him to eat.

He would say he was at his brother's house the whole night, not knowing that there were nights that I was on the phone with my sister-in-law. I heard when he got there—just minutes before heading home. After arriving home so late, he often spent hours on the couch, not coming to bed until close to 4 a.m. most nights, so my interaction with him was a maximum of an hour or two a day.

All these things I observed, making mental notes as time passed. I also journaled a lot because I needed an outlet. Of course, I argued and complained about everything, and as usual, he brushed me off and was unresponsive most times. My nagging was not the right approach either, but I didn't know what else to do. He didn't care how his actions made me feel. The more I spoke about it, the more he did it. In all my heartache, I would cry to him, but he would tell me that if I was going to cry, I shouldn't try to speak to him because he wasn't listening.

Many nights, I sat in my closet and cried non-stop while praying for God to fix my mess. I constantly told God, "I know I chose my own way once again, but I need You right now." Each time I cried out to God, He filled me with His peace and gave me strength to face another day.

We always choose our own way, and then cry out to God to bless our mess. God wants to bless us as we allow Him to lead our lives and walk in His purpose for us. It's time to start choosing God's way over our own.

My husband had moved in with me and my mother, and my mother is the type of person that doesn't keep her opinions to herself. She would make comments all the time about how he treated me and ask why he didn't spend more time with me and so on. This would make him uncomfortable and make me angry. I kept asking her not to get involved, but she couldn't help herself. She had a front seat to the show and couldn't turn a blind eye.

I felt maybe if we didn't live with my mom and had a place of our own, things would be better. I ended up in a terrible disagreement with my mother and some family members when I suggested we sell the house and split the money with my mother so everyone could get their own place. In my mind, I was willing to try anything to make this marriage work, but I wasn't thinking anything through. Every day I thank God that they fought me on that idea because I would have regretted it greatly. It probably would have cost me my relationship with my family.

During my entire marriage, I suspected my husband was cheating. I would find receipts all over the room, have girls follow me on Instagram, and see certain phone numbers on the phone bill (yes, I checked it because I was in a paranoid state that I never want to go back to). I would also hear him whisper on the phone downstairs late in the night when he thought I was sleeping. In all of this, I never felt like I had concrete evidence, even though I was almost one hundred percent sure. I would confront him over and over again with anything I found. Of course, like clockwork, the argument would end with him cursing me for searching for things. I was in a dark place, feeling like I was slowly losing myself.

There were times when we argued that I would walk out of the house in the middle of the night and sit on the sidewalk in front of my complex. He would get even more upset with me for doing that because I was putting myself in harm's way and making a scene as well. Once he barricaded the door with chairs to prevent me from leaving, so I was forced to retreat to the bedroom and cry. I was married, but it was the loneliest I have ever felt in my entire life.

My husband was usually not interested in going anywhere with me, not even on vacations. It always felt like I was pulling teeth to get him to go anywhere. The times he did come along, his face would tell the world he didn't want to be there. Trips back home to Jamaica were always separate. I was so hurt by this! He never in all our years of marriage took a trip back home with me. I would go, and then when I returned, he would go. A couple times we were there at the same time but never traveled together. Friends questioned the logic, and I had no explanation, so I made up excuses about time off or work demands or something.

I tried not to vomit my pain and frustration on everyone I spoke to. I used to be around friends and try to hide my pain from those who never knew what was going on, and I was fairly good at it. On the outside, I could smile, laugh, and have a blast with everyone; but on the inside, I felt like I was dying and in so much pain. We were moving in two different directions. Like east and west, our paths were never going to cross. A marriage cannot function without unity.

If a house is divided against itself, that house cannot stand.
Mark 3:25 (NIV)

Prayer for Married Couples

Dear gracious Heavenly Father, I come before You now in the name of Your Son Jesus Christ, and I repent of my sins. Lord, I submit my marriage to You completely. I pray for restoration, in Jesus name. I pray for an increase in love and loyalty. I pray that as a couple, we will walk in unity with You at the center of our union. Help me to plant seeds of kindness, grace, and peace, daily in my marriage. Soften the hearts of both of us, and give us compassion for one another. Let Your will be done in our lives. In Jesus' name, Amen!

Advice for Singles

If there is anything you identify while dating that is a non-negotiable for you, do not ignore it. It will be magnified in marriage. Get rid of the lie that says once you are married, things will be better. If a person doesn't see the need to change for themselves, you cannot and will not be able to change them.

Another thing is that you will eventually start picking up the bad habits because as you are around someone, you are influenced by their behavior. I was not a strong enough Christian at the time to let the light of God overpower my husband's darkness. I needed to know who I was in Christ before taking on a partner. It is better to be single and lonely than married and miserable.

Be comfortable and confident in your current status and use this time to build your relationship with Christ. As you walk with Christ in your singleness, He will give you His unexplainable joy!

*May the God of hope fill you with all joy and peace
as you trust in him, so that you may overflow with hope
by the power of the Holy Spirit.
Romans 15:13 (NIV)*

Prayer for Singles Who Are Dating

Dear gracious Heavenly Father, I come before You now in the name of Your Son Jesus Christ, and I repent of my sins. Lord, I pray that You will open my eyes to see the "red flags." Help me look for the godly qualities in my potential spouse and not just physical attributes. Give me wisdom to identify the one You sent for me and to not be distracted by the counterfeits. I submit my will to You and align my life with the purpose You have for me. In Jesus' name, Amen!

Chapter 7

The Point of No Return All Downhill from Here

In 2017, we hit what felt like the lowest point ever in our marriage, and I asked him if we could go to counseling to which he responded that he was not willing to talk about his life to a stranger. We were basically roommates by this time. When I was home, he was out, and he would return when I was sleeping. We had barely any interaction and the little we had was filled with arguments and harsh words. I became a person I didn't recognize anymore, and that got me into a deeper depression. One of my close spiritual brothers helped me one day to realize that I was being emotionally abused; I needed to make a decision. I kept telling him that I didn't believe in divorce, and I didn't want to disappoint God anymore. He reminded me that God always loves me. His grace is sufficient! I left that conversation with a lot on my mind, but I still believed that it wasn't time to give up.

I convinced my husband to take a trip with me to Detroit to spend some time with two people I met on a church mission trip years before—two of the biggest blessings of my life. He had met them previously on one of their Florida visits and clicked really well with them. I was praying that spending time with them and hearing the message preached on Sunday would stir up some change in our marriage, but my plan didn't really work. My husband was distracted for most of the trip. He was always on his phone, messaging people during dinner and walking out of the hotel room to take calls. It was very frustrating.

After our trip, things just continued along the same path. My husband fed me lies like they were food. I didn't trust a bone in his body, and my role as detective grew. His suspicious behavior one night led me to snoop in a planner he had in his laptop bag. There I found a number of greeting cards all from the same person. As I read each card, I somehow was not surprised but deeply hurt and angry. I left the cards on the couch with a note saying I wish you and her all the best. Once again, true to himself, the blame was placed on me for going through his stuff, and he refused to discuss it because I had violated his privacy. The only response I received was "She is just a friend." That was the biggest lie ever, and we both knew it.

I mentioned earlier that I forgive easily, and I don't stay angry for long. So even though I got no honest answers from that situation and the pain was still so real, I moved on with life and continued to be his wife, doing what I had to do. Despite comments from my close friends that they would stop doing regular wifely tasks to spite him, I insisted that I was going to continue to show love and play my role because that is what God would want from me.

My detective work didn't stop though. I found out the full name and background of this girl, all without having to look too far. With all the information I had, I was a danger to myself, stressing my mental health as I considered what to do with this information. Should I call her? No, that's not me. I wasn't married to her, and she owed me no explanation. Should I confront him? Nope, that would just lead to another argument and then nowhere. I was spiraling out of control with confusion.

I ended up enrolling in marital counseling with a Christian counselor by myself. Despite how silly it felt initially, I knew I needed help, and I had to get it by any means possible. My counselor started by having me work through my past hurts so I could receive healing. This was important because these had not been addressed yet were still an issue deep down. God can heal you and renew your mind, but I genuinely believe in getting professional Christian help as well; it is very necessary. God uses His people to minister to one another and help in the healing process.

One Sunday evening, I was cooking while my husband took a nap on the couch. I was in a state of mind that I cannot explain. I cried out to the Lord and told Him to give me something that would allow me to walk away from this marriage and not feel guilty about it. I had made so many mistakes up to this point in my life that I didn't want to move until I felt the Lord saying it was ok. Within an hour, the evidence of his cheating and the push I needed to say goodbye to my marriage basically fell into my lap. It was unbelievable! I didn't have to do anything but listen. This flood of information continued into the following day, and all the pieces I had gathered over some time came together perfectly, making complete sense. In the midst of the heartache, I felt peace come over me like never before.

That night, before I could get a chance to confront my husband, he came home from work "guns blazing." He cursed and shouted and almost blew a fuse. He acted in a way I had never seen, and for the first time in the years of knowing him, I felt slightly in fear for my life. He didn't touch me, but his demeanor was something I'd never seen in all the years of knowing him. Throughout that entire encounter, I was not my usual self, going head to head with him. I was calm—so calm that it upset him even more! I was in disbelief with myself as well, but as I said before, I had received an inexplicable peace about everything that was going on that day.

And the peace of God, which transcends all understanding, will guard your hearts and your minds in Christ Jesus.
Philippians 4:7 (NIV)

THE POINT OF NO RETURN

My husband's approach to the whole situation made it easy for me to make up my mind to finally file for a divorce. If he had tried to talk things out with me, or even offered to go to counseling to mend our relationship, things might have been different. Also, if he were even a little remorseful, I would have forgiven him. He had zero remorse and that was hard to deal with. I spoke to two of the spiritual leaders in my life, and after much prayer, I continued to feel at peace about my decision to leave.

Let me just be clear: I'm not saying that if your marriage is rocky, divorce is the answer. The Lord hates divorce. I spent years in prayer and fasting, and I sought godly counsel before getting to the point of divorce. I waited for the Lord to let me know through many confirmations that it was ok to leave. As I mentioned earlier, I never wanted to walk out of God's will again, so I had to be sure. The Lord hears our prayers, and He will answer and provide relief in whichever way He sees fit. Don't make a move without consulting the Holy Spirit!

The righteous cry out, and the Lord hears them;
he delivers them from all their troubles. The Lord is close to the
brokenhearted and saves those who are crushed in spirit.
Psalm 34:17-18 (NIV)

The divorce process was like a runaway train to hell. He made sure to make my life miserable. Remember earlier when I said I would ask God why He never gave me the child He promised, and

I would get upset and cry? Well, in the middle of the divorce chaos, I had to humbly go to the Lord and ask for forgiveness. I realized how much more difficult my divorce would have been had there been a child or children in the mix.

God never makes mistakes, and everything works in His perfect time, not mine.

I tried to do the divorce the simple way, where we would settle without involving lawyers, but my husband tore the papers up in front of my face and threw them all over the living room. This made me furious, and that night ended up with us in a heated argument, as usual. By this time, we were both acting out of character. I received threats from him, and his family treated me like I was the one at fault. Once again, my friends and family pleaded with me to fight the process. All I could say was that no matter what happened, he would never truly win in the end. My God would restore what he had taken, plus more. I just wanted it all to be over.

We unofficially separated in April of 2018, and he fully moved out of the house by the first week of June that year. Knowing that he no longer lived in the house felt strange at first, but his physical absence was nothing new. I remember telling people that he must have been preparing me for this day by allowing me to basically be alone in the marriage all these years. I used to open the empty closet and cry because I couldn't believe my marriage was really over. I had fought for this to work, and once again, that feeling of being a failure reared its ugly head.

After a year, all was finalized; it was the best day of my life! So much weight was lifted off my shoulders. I felt FREE!

My marital counseling sessions turned into healing sessions during the divorce process. My counselor and I worked through my feelings of failure, embarrassment, pain, anger, betrayal, and hopelessness. She encouraged me to date myself which felt a little weird at first. I went out to the movies and lunch or dinner by myself. I always wondered what people around me were thinking. Did they think I was pathetic or lonely being by myself? During my first movie alone, I sat beside a family and leaned over a little in my seat toward them when the lights were on in the theater to give the impression that I was with them. Afterward, I looked back at that night and laughed at myself! Subsequent times were better. It took some time for me to block out the negative thoughts and enjoy my own company, but it was a worthy exercise, and I'm glad I committed to the process. Eventually, the counselor told me that I no longer needed the sessions. I was finally happy, whole, and healthy in all aspects, or so we thought. Looking back, I was finished with all she could help me with. Now it was up to me to take what I learned and apply it.

Lessons Learned

I learned a lot from my five years of marriage and realized that I had been given so many signs from day one that I totally ignored. During the dating period, there were a number of red flags, but like most women, I felt things would change once we were married. That is the biggest misconception ever! It is more likely that these things will intensify. I also felt that once we were married, he would be with me, and the distance-related issues would disappear. Wrong again! After getting married, the flags kept popping up everywhere and we somehow got more distant.

Even though I knew from early on that the marriage would probably not work out, I still pushed and fought for my marriage—a fight that I felt I was in all alone. Imagine being in a boxing ring with yourself for years. After a while, you get frustrated, you feel foolish, as if you are wasting time doing nothing. I continued to be the best wife I knew how to be. When my husband would voice his opinions about what I was doing wrong, I consciously made an effort to change because I wanted to make it work. Let me be clear: I wasn't perfect, but I tried my best and gave it my all. No one is perfect, and a perfect marriage is just two imperfect people coming together and striving to make things work. It's all about meeting each other where you are and working together. Communication is key, and I'm sure most of you are tired of hearing that, but without communication, a marriage will fail.

The number one thing though, is having God in the center of the marriage. He is the head of the relationship; as both people draw closer to Him, they draw closer to each other. This is why the Bible says not to be unequally yoked. It is impossible to function as a team. Simple things like going to church become arguments, and those little arguments brew into bigger things that eat away at the connection you once had.

> Don't team up with those who are unbelievers. How can righteousness be a partner with wickedness? How can light live with darkness?
> II Corinthians 6:14 (NLT)

> Yet you, Lord, are our Father.
> We are the clay; you are the potter;
> we are all the work of your hand.
> Isaiah 64:8 (NIV)

There is a blessing in being broken. What you think is rejection is redirection.

There is a God who sees you. He knows you by name, and He knows where to find you in your brokenness. Best of all, He's never going to let you go. The Potter wants to put us back together again. No matter how broken we are, God will always be with us and will mend our broken pieces.

Prayer for Brokenness

Dear gracious Heavenly Father, I pray in the name of Jesus Christ of Nazareth. Lord, I want to thank You for never leaving me nor forsaking me. I place the broken pieces of my heart and life in Your hands, Father. You are the Potter, and I will be the clay. Mend my broken heart and mold me to what You intend for me to be. I surrender all to You, God. Please send Your Holy Spirit to comfort me during this season. Forgive me for stepping out of Your will, time and time again. Thank You that in my weakness, I am strong because the power of Christ rests upon me. Thank You for Your unlimited grace and mercy in my life. In Jesus' name, Amen!

Chapter 8

Life After Divorce

I t was April 30, 2019. I was now free, single, and disengaged, but was I really free? Legally, I was. But what about emotionally and spiritually? Divorce was never something I imagined for myself, especially at thirty-three years old. I kept blaming myself for stepping out of God's will and doing things my way. I still felt some of the weight of being tied to this man that caused so much pain and heartache in my life. Then, all the questions came at me like a flood. Did I do the right thing? Did God really give me peace about it, or did I just imagine that? I am getting older, and now I have to start all over again! God promised me my child; when will that happen? How am I going to date now? I haven't done this in years! My emotions were all over the place.

However, instead of closing myself off from the world and wallowing in my pain and disappointment, I drew closer to the number one source of my strength: Jesus. My Bishop from Jamaica had started doing weekly Instagram live services, and I made sure to be present for almost all of them. I got more serious with my time in the Word and prayer. I told God that I never wanted to step out of His will again.

I signed up for a mentorship program, and it was perfect timing! I was broken but trying to tell myself I was fine, even though I knew I wasn't. Through the program, I was able to get the spiritual healing I needed. Something I hadn't realized was that I had to deal with "soul ties." I was still tied up with all the men I had ever been involved with throughout my life! In order for me to step into my new self and be fully healed, those ties had to be severed. That deliverance was received through the mentorship program.

I was not short of support. My ministry family in Jamaica, my local church family, and my friends and family all supported me and played major roles in the healing process. As always, you will have the person who would come along and say you should have done this or that to spite your ex-husband, but I just smiled and said I'm not like that.

Throughout this time, I still had a small void in my heart. My ex-husband and I hadn't spoken for months, and whenever we did, it wasn't pleasant. I am not a person that is capable of malice, no matter what is done to me, so it hurt to know we couldn't get along, especially because I knew he was holding on to lies about me.

LIFE AFTER DIVORCE

The first time we had to meet up after the divorce was at the bank to remove his name from my accounts. I still had some resentment inside. I barely looked at him during the process, even though he attempted to speak to me and ask how I was. We had one more bank to visit together and that visit came months later, in November of 2019; we could not agree on a meet-up time prior to that. Waiting in the lobby of the bank for him to show up was nerve racking! As I said, we barely spoke and a couple days prior, his brother threatened me and told me to stay away from his son—that's a story for another time. So needless to say, I didn't know what to expect.

Each time the bank door opened, my heart skipped a beat. I had not felt this nervous in a long time. I wanted to clear the tension between us but didn't know how to. He wasn't the easiest person to speak to, and technically, I wasn't obligated to succumb to the stress of trying to make amends. When he arrived, I couldn't look at him, but I said hi. We took care of the transactions and walked out together.

Upon leaving, he asked if I was doing ok. I finally looked at him and said, "Yes, I'm doing great," which was mostly true. Apart from my tension with him, all else was going well. Then I mentioned his brother and what he had said to me, and that started the conversation. We stood in the parking lot for four hours and spoke about almost everything.

We had the conversation that we should have had two years prior when this all started. He finally listened to me. He realized that all he had believed was a lie, that he was blaming me for things I didn't do. At one point, the relief that I finally felt made my eyes tear up. I immediately started speaking to myself to suck it up because I didn't want him to see me cry.

After our talk that day, I could really say that I was finally FREE! I got my closure, and I could live and be complete again. We spoke subsequently, and in another lengthy conversation, we were both able to identify areas where we were each at fault. He was emotionally absent throughout the marriage, and that was evident when he would ignore my issues and my tears. He apologized to me and admitted that he was selfish and let his ego take control. This was a huge step for him. I appreciated that talk very much because we were very vulnerable with each other. I also got what I was longing for: he finally realized and took responsibility for the major role he played.

It's funny how life works. Many people would have just cut their ex-spouse out of their life, saying they are "dead to me." But that leaves you with an area of unforgiveness that will eat you up little by little and block your blessings. Prior to our conversation that day, I kept telling people I forgave my ex-husband, that there were no bad feelings. But if I were to be completely honest with myself, my true and complete forgiveness didn't come until that day in the parking lot.

LIFE AFTER DIVORCE

I can now speak to my ex and have no ill feelings. We came to a place of reconciliation. This is an example of how even in all the hurt and pain, we can still love one another and forgive. I wish him all the best in life and pray that he will find his way back to the Lord someday. To get through this life, we all need Jesus; and in Him, we need to receive the ultimate gift of eternal life. This world is a scary place, and I've learned how one decision without God can turn your life upside down.

"Therefore, if you are offering your gift at the altar and there remember that your brother or sister has something against you, leave your gift there in front of the altar. First go and be reconciled to them; then come and offer your gift.
Matthew 5:23-24 (NIV)

If your brother or sister sins, go and point out their fault, just between the two of you. If they listen to you, you have won them over.
Matthew 18:15 (NIV)

I started dating again after our split, and I must say, this dating world isn't easy! However, I am more aware of what I need to look out for and more able to walk away when the red flags appear. I have made some new friends through the experience, and each of them has taught me something new, even though they may not realize they have. Each day is a learning experience for me, especially since I haven't dated in eight years, nor have I dated fully as a Christian. This new road is difficult and dying to my flesh isn't easy. But it is something that is important to me and what the Lord expects. I am looking forward to what God has in store for me.

I found Iyanla Vanzant's 4 "P's" one day and thought it would be great to share. Iyanla is an American inspirational speaker, lawyer, life coach, and so much more! Her 4 "P's" are a good summary of what women want in a relationship.

The 4 "P's" are

1. Protect - Give a sense of security
2. Provide - Financially, Emotionally
3. Perform - Duties as a man/husband being the head of the household
4. Please – Physically

I would add one more—Prayer. A praying man is absolutely important. A man who submits to Christ shows that he is someone you can submit to.

In the end, no matter how many checklists we come up with, the Holy Spirit must be our guide and let us know when the right one comes along.

LIFE AFTER DIVORCE

For his anger lasts only a moment, but his favor lasts a lifetime;
weeping may stay for the night,
but rejoicing comes in the morning.
Psalm 30:5 (NIV)

Peace I leave with you; my peace I give you.
I do not give to you as the world gives.
Do not let your hearts be troubled and do not be afraid.
John 14:27 (NIV)

Prayer of Thanksgiving

Dear gracious Heavenly Father, I want to thank you for wiping the tears from my eyes and giving me true joy. Thank You for always being there with me every step of the way. Thank You for Your peace. I can rest knowing that You are in control. Thank You that I can never go too far from You. Thank You for loving me and blessing me, in spite of my mess. I praise Your Holy name. In Jesus' name I pray, Amen!

Chapter 9

My Renewed Walk with Christ

There's no doubt about it
I'm on my way home
I'm not yet where I'm going
but I'm a long way from where I was...
I'm not going back,
Never going back
How amazing to know that
We've only just begun
Yeah, we've only just begun
I'll keep pressing on, I'll keep going strong
I'll keep singing the same song...

Excerpt from We The Kingdom's "No Doubt About It"
Songwriters: Ed Cash, Scott Cash, Franni Cash, Martin Cash,
Andrew Bergthold, and Kyle Briskin

As I have heard so many times, this life is a marathon and not a sprint. We fall down, and we get back up. The idea is to keep moving forward. After so many years of doing things my way, even though I called myself a Christian, I have finally decided to truly submit to the will and way of the Lord.

Disclaimer: This doesn't mean I will be perfect and never make another mistake again. It just means I will be obedient to the voice of God, and if I stumble, I will run to Him and repent. The most amazing thing about God is that despite our sins, He is merciful and shows us compassion when we humbly approach His throne, confess our sins, and repent. For many years, I lived being influenced by the ways of the world. I kept doing my wrongs and took God's forgiveness and grace for granted. I abused the unconditional love He has for me, and that's where many of us live at this moment. While I'm so grateful that He never gave up on me, I am also grateful that my time didn't run out before it was too late to turn my life around. He gave me beauty for my ashes.

God says He will—

> ...Provide for those who grieve in Zion—
> to bestow on them a crown of beauty
> instead of ashes,
> the oil of joy
> instead of mourning,
> and a garment of praise
> instead of a spirit of despair.

MY RENEWED WALK WITH CHRIST

They will be called oaks of righteousness,
a planting of the Lord
for the display of his splendor.
Isaiah 61:3 (NIV)

Today, if you are stuck in a cycle like I was, I want you to know these truths:

1. God loves you and that will never change.

   Who shall separate us from the love of Christ?
   Shall trouble or hardship or persecution or famine
   or nakedness or danger or sword?
   Romans 8:35 (NIV)

2. You are never alone.

   If I go up to the heavens, you are there;
   if I make my bed in the depths, you are there.
   Psalm 139:8 (NIV)

3. There is no such thing as an unforgivable sin.

   If we confess our sins, he is faithful and just and will forgive us our
   sins and purify us from all unrighteousness.
   1 John 1:9 (NIV)

Don't put off for tomorrow what can be done right now. We never know what tomorrow will bring. Confess your sins to God and give Him control. Welcome the Holy Spirit into your life. Say the repentance prayer.

For it is with your heart that you believe and are justified,
and it is with your mouth that you profess your faith
and are saved.
Romans 10:10 (NIV)

Repentance Prayer

Dear Heavenly Father, I (your name) am a sinner, and I repent of all my sins. I confess with my mouth and believe in my heart that Jesus Christ is Your Son. I acknowledge that Jesus Christ died on the cross for my sins and resurrected on the third day and will return for me. I now invite Jesus Christ into my heart as my personal Lord and Savior. I praise you because today my name is written in the Lamb's Book of Life. In Jesus' name I pray, Amen!

Date: _____

God wants us to live a fulfilled life in Him. We will definitely have troubles because we are living in a broken world, but His Word reassures us that we can always lean on Him.

Cast all your anxiety on him because he cares for you.
1 Peter 5:7 (NIV)

"Come to me, all you who are weary and burdened, and I will give you rest. Take my yoke upon you and learn from me, for I am gentle and humble in heart, and you will find rest for your souls. For my yoke is easy and my burden is light."
Matthew 11:28-30 (NIV)

It is a common misconception that being a Christian is boring and that God doesn't want us to have fun and enjoy life. Let me be honest with you; I used to think that too. But ever since I got serious about my journey with Christ, I have never been happier and never felt so complete. Troubles still come my way, but the difference is that I have God to fight my battles for me.

The thief does not come except to steal, and to kill, and to destroy.
I have come that they may have life,
and that they may have it more abundantly.
John 10:10 (NKJV)

MY RENEWED WALK WITH CHRIST

Turning your life around isn't a simple task, but with Christ all things are possible.

> I can do all things through Christ who strengthens me.
> Philippians 4:13 (NKJV)

Also, there are a few things I do that help me stay focused and can probably help you as well. Adapt the following to your situation:

1. Pray Always - for any and every reason. Create a habit of consistent communication with the Father.

> Rejoice always, pray without ceasing, in everything give thanks; for this is the will of God in Christ Jesus for you.
> I Thessalonians 5:16-18 (NKJV)

2. Read the Word - Set a specific time in each day to do a devotional and study God's Word.

> Remain in me, and I will remain in you. For a branch cannot produce fruit if it is severed from the vine, and you cannot be fruitful unless you remain in me. John 15:4 (NLT)

3. Speak Life - words frame your world. They energize and build us up or create doubt. What you speak determines who you are.

> The tongue has the power of life and death,
> and those who love it will eat its fruit.
> Proverbs 18:21 (NIV)

4. Journal - write prayers to God about your days and how you are feeling. Writing can be very therapeutic. It is an outlet to release things instead of keeping them inside.

5. Listen to gospel music – This feeds your soul with the right thing.

6. Watch sermons on YouTube.

7. Mirror Messages – Put up Post-it notes with encouraging Bible verses in places you will notice like on the bathroom mirror.

8. Connect with a Bible-believing ministry.

9. Beach Walks – notice the sunrise and sunset. Take in the beauty of God's creation and use that peaceful time to speak to Him.

10. Join a small group - It is important to be vulnerable and be in community with others. A small group gives you the opportunity to be who you are, get support, and give support to others. In a small group you can empty yourself of pride as you serve and learn from each other.

And let us not neglect our meeting together, as some people do, but encourage one another,
especially now that the day of his return is drawing near.
Hebrews 10:25 (NLT)

More Lessons Learned

No matter how many times I walked away from God, the Holy Spirit brought me back to Him and His grace covered me. I do not know how to keep malice. I am always the one to break the silence. I've been known to forgive others easily. I honestly believe this is because I know that I daily fall short and sin, but God constantly forgives me. So, who am I to hold a grudge?

> Bear with each other and forgive one another if any of you has a grievance against someone. Forgive as the Lord forgave you.
> Colossians 3:13 (NIV)

God's mercy toward us is endless, even if we choose the wrong way and ignore His warnings. Once we turn to Him, He will get us back on track, but it is so much easier to listen and obey the first time He speaks. Getting off track and out of God's will is always painful and comes with consequences. We do make mistakes in life, but we can reduce those mistakes drastically if we earnestly seek God's will in all we do and obey His instructions.

Conclusion

I know there are many people out there who have similar stories or worse than the ones I shared in this book. Looking back at all I have gone through, I genuinely believe that there is such a great purpose for my life. The enemy has been fighting for my life for so long, trying to stop me from fulfilling my purpose and living completely sold out for Christ. He would only be this concerned because he knows the damage I can cause to his plans for this world.

It is the same for you. You may have made a wrong turn over and over again. Every time you make up your mind to follow Jesus, the enemy throws a wrench in your plans, and you fall. We are not perfect, and we won't be as long as we are living in the world, but we have to get up daily and stay prepared for the enemy's attacks. Don't let him catch you off guard or you will slip. I always thought I was so strong. I thought I could resist the devil with ease, but as you have read, I failed numerous times. I do know that without going through a process, there will be no growth, so I am grateful for the trials. God has turned them around for my good and allowed me to grow. God has truly been so faithful!

Therefore, since we have been justified through faith, we have peace with God through our Lord Jesus Christ, through whom we have gained access by faith into this grace in which we now stand. And we boast in the hope of the glory of God. Not only so, but we also glory in our sufferings, because we know that suffering produces perseverance; perseverance, character; and character, hope. And hope does not put us to shame, because God's love has been poured out into our hearts through the Holy Spirit, who has been given to us.
Romans 5:1-5 (NIV)

(Verse 1)
I love You Lord
Oh, your mercy never fails me
All my days, I've been held in Your hands
From the moment that I wake up
Until I lay my head
I will sing of the goodness of God

(Chorus)
All my life You have been faithful
All my life You have been so, so good
With every breath that I am able
I will sing of the goodness of God
(Verse 2)
I love Your voice
You have led me through the fire
In darkest nights
You are close like no other

CONCLUSION

I've known You as a father
I've known You as a friend
I have lived in the goodness of God

Bridge
Your goodness is running after, it's running after me
Your goodness is running after, it's running after me
With my life laid down, I'm surrendered now,
I give You everything
Your goodness is running after, it's running after me

"Goodness of God" - Bethel Music, Jenn Johnson

Always keep God's words engraved in your heart and mind. Study this Book of Instruction continually. Meditate on it day and night so you will be sure to obey everything written in it. Only then will you prosper and succeed in all you do.
Joshua 1:8 (NLT)

I have hidden your word in my heart
that I might not sin against you.
Psalms 119:11 (NIV)

Avoid situations where you will be tempted, no matter how strong you think you are. It is better to be safe than sorry.

Submit yourselves, then, to God. Resist the devil,
and he will flee from you.
James 4:7 (NIV)

God sometimes strips us of everything we are depending on to cause us to depend on Him. We come to the Father empty of ourselves, and He fills us. Allow God to fill you today. He is ready to renew you.

> Therefore, if anyone is in Christ, he is a new creation.
> The old has passed away; behold, the new has come.
> II Corinthians 5:17 (ESV)

> It was good for me to be afflicted
> so that I might learn your decrees
> Psalm 119:71 (NIV)

I want you to walk away from this book knowing that Jesus loves you—flaws and all!

Affirmation:
> I can walk unashamed because GOD LOVES ME!

Journal and Prayers

_____

_____

_____

_____

_____

_____

_____

_____

_____

_____

_____

_____

_____

_____

THE TRUTH BEHIND MY SMILE

_____

_____

_____

_____

_____

_____

_____

_____

_____

_____

_____

_____

_____

_____

_____

_____

_____

_____

_____

_____

_____

_____

THE TRUTH BEHIND MY SMILE

_____

_____

_____

_____

_____

_____

_____

_____

_____

_____

_____

_____

_____

_____

_____

_____

_____

_____

_____

_____

_____

_____

_____

_____

JOURNAL AND PRAYERS

_____

_____

_____

_____

_____

_____

_____

_____

_____

_____

_____

_____

_____

_____

_____

_____

_____

_____

_____

_____

_____

_____

About the Author

Justine A. Cohen was born and raised in Kingston, Jamaica, and moved to the United States in her early 20s where she currently resides in South Florida.

She earned her bachelor's degree in Accounting at the University of Technology, Jamaica, and went on to acquire her MBA in Accounting at Florida Atlantic University. She is a Certified Public Accountant and has had a successful career in the Accounting/Finance field for over fourteen years. She is also certified as an Early Childhood Educator, holding a Director credential. Her passion is early childhood education, specifically reaching the less fortunate and helping persons find healing through truth.

As you can see, her current career path is quite different from her passion, but she makes it work. Justine is a woman of God who has a heart for those who have lost hope; she believes her story can help guide them back to the hope found in God.

Her life verse is:

> See, I am doing a new thing!
> Now it springs up; do you not perceive it?
> I am making a way in the wilderness
> and streams in the wasteland.
> Isaiah 43:19 (NIV)

She believes that the best is yet to come and is excited to see how God will use her for His glory.

To find out more about what Justine is doing, you can follow her on the following social media platform:

IG: @findhealing_thrutruth